Christmas Holiday Joy

Silvia Sama-Lambiv

Christmas Holiday Joy

Dedication

This book is dedicated to The Almighty God.

Secondly, I dedicate this book to my husband,
Dr. Wanyu Lambiv, and to our beloved children for
their steadfast love, encouragement and support.

I also dedicate this book to men, women and children
who believe in the birth of Jesus Christ!

To everyone who celebrates Christmas and beliefs,
and contributes to the Christmas Miracle. Thank you
all and may God bless you and your families during
this special time of the year.

We are a blessing to each other,
and we love Christmas!

Lastly, I dedicate this book to all those who have lost
loved ones during this pandemic and loved ones they
will miss at Christmas.

SCHOOL

My name is Joseph and it is the last day of school before the Christmas holidays. We are all excited to go home. I will miss my friends but Christmas is my favorite holiday.

Last night, the school Christmas party was magical. We all wore our costumes for the play, followed by carolling as the audience applauded. I'm looking forward to going to the Christmas market. It will be fun.

I cannot wait for Christmas day to be here!

It is a frosty morning. There are only five days until Christmas. and we are traveling to the big Christmas market. It is a long drive, so we have snacks, water and a flask of tea for the trip. We are going to stop at my favorite restaurant at the market for lunch. I love the cookies.

Last night, we went to our city's Christmas Tree Lighting and Christmas Parade. It was so much fun to see Santa's caravan arrive with toys for all the children. My parents always support our city's Christmas Toy drive.

I love the Christmas spirit of sharing.

Baking cookies at Christmas is one of my family's Christmas traditions. Every year we bake lots of cookies for our local church bake sale and for the homeless community who find shelter at the community centers in our city.

My mom tells us that we must be grateful for everything we have. She always reminds us that it is very important to share what we have with other people who are less fortunate.

My mom makes the best cookies and we love to eat them ...

Hmmm, yummy, yummy, these cookies are delicious.

My family loves the Christmas holidays.
Another Christmas tradition my family
enjoys is playing in the snow and taking
sleigh rides. Mom and dad always take
time off to spend the holidays with us.

The best part about having fun in the snow
is drinking hot cocoa when we go inside.

Early this morning, we went to the farm and
my brothers and I helped dad to pick out
the Christmas tree. It was a fun ride and we
listened to Christmas carols on the radio all
the way.

I love playing in the snow.

Putting-up the Christmas trees and decorations is the most special night of the Christmas holidays. We get to put a tree and decorations in every room in our home as we listen and dance to Christmas carols.

Every family in our neighborhood puts up decorations outside their homes too. It is magical, the lights are so bright and beautiful.

When the Christmas trees and decorations are up, we have a little contest for the best Christmas carol dancer. The winner gets to pick the Christmas movie for the night.

I have never won the dance contest but **my favorite Christmas movie is Rudolf the Red-Nosed Reindeer.**

Going shopping at the mall and taking a family photo is another one of our family's Christmas traditions. At the mall you can hear the Salvation Army Red kettle bell ringing for donations.

While mom shops, we love to watch other shoppers as they go about their business. Everyone seems to be in a rush.

There are many discount sales at this time of the year and we get to try on some sweaters or pants in the store before mom makes the purchase.

Santa Claus makes Christmas special for children.

Santa's Workshop
ELECTRONIC
SHOP
SHOP
SALE!
SALE!
50%
OOD

During this Christmas mall experience, we get to dress up in our new outfits and go to Santa's Winter photobooth.

Here Santa's elves get us ready to meet Santa and then take the family photo. There are always many people in the queue, but mom usually schedules our photoshoot way in advance so we do not have to wait for a long time.

A visit to Santa's Worskshop is amazing and fun.

Unto US a Child Jesus is Born

We always attend the Christmas Eve Mass at our local church. The church is beautifully decorated with lights and Christmas trees everywhere – even in the restrooms.

The congregation is beautifully dressed and seated on benches, surrounded by Christmas trees and decorations. It's a heavenly feeling when the choir sings all my favorite Christmas carols. I just love Christmas. I love listening to the preaching about the birth of baby Jesus.

After the mass, we visit the manger scene at the front of the church where they recreate the scene from the Bible when baby Jesus was born in Bethlehem. We can see baby Jesus, his parents, the Blessed Virgin Mary and Saint Joseph, the shepherds with their sheep and the three wise men who followed the star to the place where baby Jesus was born, bringing Him gifts of gold, frankincense and myrrh. We always say a family prayer to baby Jesus before leaving the church.

The Christmas Miracle, Jesus is born.

Samuel, my older brother, is always the first to wake up on Christmas morning. He runs to wake us.

"I have been nice this year. I wonder what Santa brought me for Christmas," says Samuel.

"I don't know about that," Paul interrupts. "Quick, let's go downstairs and find out."

Our parents usually take us to the mall just before the Thanksgiving holiday and help us mail our Christmas letters to Santa Claus in the North Pole.

We love to pray and send letters to Santa Claus (Saint Nicholas).

MERRY
Christmas

We love dressing up for the Christmas day dinner that is served from noon till the end of the day. There is always so much to eat. Mom wakes up early to bake the turkey, stuffing and vegetables. We all help peel the potatoes and set the table.

We eat and make merry as we listen and dance to Christmas carols all day long.

My favorite Christmas carol is Jingle Bells.

MERRY
Christmas

The day after Christmas is boxing day, it is an old English tradition. We are having breakfast and snow is falling outside. It is so beautiful, I want to go build a snowman.

As a family tradition this is the time, we gather and talk about the year in perspective and

make plans for the new year.

HAPPY NEW YEAR
MERRY
Christmas

This is the best evening after Christmas Eve when we get to watch TV and see the ball drop in Times Square to ring in the New year.

As a family, this is the time we gather to share a family hug and drink to the new year with hope and faith.

My brothers and I are looking forward to returning to school and playing with our friends.

Our parents always share a kiss at midnight ... eeeewwww.

About the author

Silvia Sama-Lambiv was a contributing author of several articles in Y'ello Magazine while she worked for MTNC, the African Telecommunications giant in Cameroon where she started her career as a writer. She has also written for a popular UK based print and online magazine. She holds a Bachelor's degree from the University of Douala in Cameroon, a Certificate in Intellectual Property 'from WIPO, World Intellectual Property Organization in Geneva, Switzerland and other Information Technology Certifications. She speaks five languages. Christmas Holiday Joy' is her first Children's illustrated book. She is also the author of 'Christmas Holiday Joy (Coloring Experience)', 'Color Me American' and 'Color Me Global Citizen' (Coloring book) soon to be published. She is a member of several Writer Groups and Forums on social media and linkedin. When she is not writing, she works full time as an Information Technology Professional, a Philanthropist, as well as a volunteer for many causes relevant to her Catholic Christian lifestyle. Silvia Sama-Lambiv grew up in several West African cities including Bamenda, Kumba, Yaounde, Limbe, Garoua, Kumbo and Douala in The Republic of Cameroon before moving to Europe where she joined her husband in Lausanne, Switzerland. She later moved to the United States over a decade ago where she resides with her husband and three children. In her spare time, Silvia enjoys devotional books, music, traveling, cooking, biking and hiking.